ASTROLOGY FOR DOGS

by Simone Reyes

Cover Illustration by Design Dynamics
Typography by Marketforce

Published by Great Quotations Publishing Co.,
Glendale Heights, IL

Library of Congress Catalog Card Number: 98-71849

ISBN 1-56245-344-0

Printed in U.S.A.

2

Dedicated to all the animals in the world who have no voice, no choice. And to the following organizations: PETA (People For the Ethical Treatment of Animals)-the Leader of the Pack, LCA (Last Chance for Animals), the ALF (Animal Liberation Front), (the legendary) Activists For Animals, The Brigitte Bardot Foundation, The Doris Day Animal League, The Milarepa Fund, Being Kind, Greenpeace, PCRM (Physicians Committee For Responsible Medicine), The Fund for Animals, Farm Sanctuary and countless others for *always* being on the side of right.

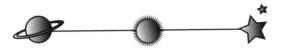

Introduction

As responsible dog guardians, we strive to give our companion animals all the love and support they deserve. Therefore, looking into "unconventional" methods, such as Astrology, to communicate with "man's best friend" is actually quite a logical step. It is my heartfelt wish that your dog will walk hand in paw with you throughout the duration of your lives. I hope for you that you may feel secure in knowing that the power of the zodiac walks with you forever educating, enlightening, nurturing and protecting you in her light.

4

* You will notice that I have used the words "he" and "she" interchangeably when referring to dogs, except in instances where I am being gender specific.

Quotation:

"Can't decide between a Great Dane, Scottish Terrier or Poodle? Have them all, adopt a mutt!"

    -ASPCA

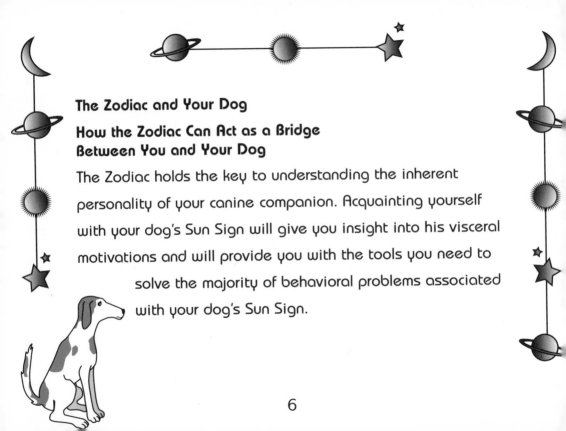

The Zodiac and Your Dog

How the Zodiac Can Act as a Bridge Between You and Your Dog

The Zodiac holds the key to understanding the inherent personality of your canine companion. Acquainting yourself with your dog's Sun Sign will give you insight into his visceral motivations and will provide you with the tools you need to solve the majority of behavioral problems associated with your dog's Sun Sign.

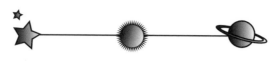

Knowing your dog's Sun Sign will help you determine if your dog is people-friendly, has difficulty relating to other dogs in "dog run" type situations, is more likely to be tolerant of children, is more inclined to be a lap dog, etc.

The insight you will gain by knowing the Sun Sign of your best four legged friend will enhance the relationship you share with your dog by allowing you to understand his/her basic instincts and behavior.

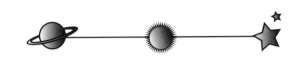

Sun Signs and Their Meanings

A dog's Sun Sign begins to make its influence felt at about six weeks of age, when a puppy is beginning to move from puppy-hood into dog-hood. It is during this phase that puppies begin to view themselves as independent beings in the world. By three months of age, the Sun Sign will be in full effect. Once you have determined your canine's Sun Sign, you will be flooded with important information that only the planets can reveal about your pup.

8

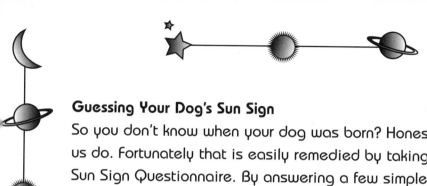

Guessing Your Dog's Sun Sign

So you don't know when your dog was born? Honestly, few of us do. Fortunately that is easily remedied by taking the Canine Sun Sign Questionnaire. By answering a few simple questions, you will be on the road to knowing your dog's Sun Sign.

9

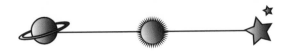

CANINE SUN SIGN QUESTIONNAIRE

This is a simple test which will help you determine the Sun Sign that your dog was born under. There are two parts to the test (Section 1 and Section 2). Section 1 will ask you to guess which element (Fire, Earth, Air or Water) best characterizes your dog, and Section 2 will ask you to keep a score card by answering various questions about your canine. Once both sections are completed, you can match the dog's element and the dog's score to determine the Sun Sign!

10

Section 1: Guessing Your Dog's Element

Check off the groups of adjectives that best describe your canine pal. Limit your choice to one grouping. This will determine if he or she is a Fire, Earth, Air or Water sign:

-FIRE: Enthusiastic, Brave, Peppy
(tornado dog)

-EARTH: Grounded, Lazy, Self-involved
(basic lazy bones)

-AIR: Loud, Independent, Curious
(woof, woof, WOOF!)

-WATER: Shy, Introverted, Gentle
(angel baby)

11

Section 2: Targeting Your Dog's Personality

(add up your score)

1. Decide which statement could best be spoken by your pup:

• "I'm the type of dog who likes to smell around, I'm the wanderer, the dog wander...I sniff around, around, around."

0 points

• "All by myself...I like to be all by myself... love my human, but I'm the James Dean type of loner dog."

1 point

• "Karma, Karma, Karma Chameleon Dog, my moods come and go, I'm a changin' dog."

2 points

12

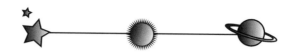

2. Choose which celebrity your pooch most closely mirrors in mannerisms:

Rocker Courtney Love or Shock Jock Howard Stern

0 points

Mystical Stevie Nicks or The Boss Bruce Springsteen

1 points

Funny Gal Roseanne or Late Show's David Letterman

2 points

13

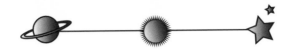

3. Decide which personality portrait your dog falls under:

Personality #1: Playful, Aggressive, Active

0 points

Personality #2: Relentless, Stubborn, Exhausting

10 points

Personality #3: Wishy-Washy, Volatile, Whimsical

20 points

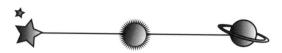

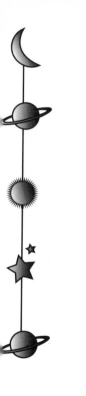

4 . Which type of music does your dog respond most favorably to?

Heavy Metal, Alternative or Rap - the louder the better

0 points

Easy Listening or Country - sappy songs

1 point

Elevator Music, Gregorian Chants, Salsa - you name it

2 points

5. What is your dog's favorite game?

Run, catch, kill, bury, dig up, repeat-
with a chew toy, not an animal
0 points

Fetch

1 point

Tripping you - accidentally, of course

2 points

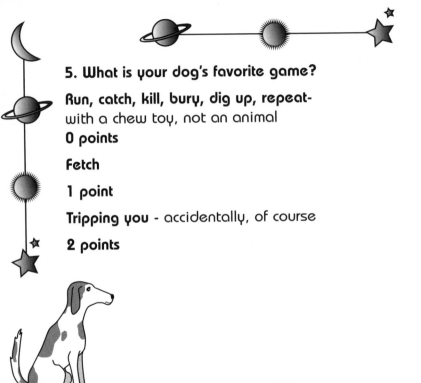

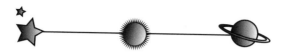

Part 3: EVALUATION

Add up your score to determine if your dog is a TYPE A personality, TYPE B personality or TYPE C personality:

1-10 points   **TYPE A**

10-20 points   **TYPE B**

20-30 points   **TYPE C**

Now that you have determined which personality type your dog is, go back to Part 1 of this questionnaire and match your dog's element to the following chart:

Fire + Type A	= ARIES
Fire + Type B	= LEO
Fire + Type C	= SAGITTARIUS
Earth + Type A	= CAPRICORN
Earth + Type B	= TAURUS
Earth + Type C	= VIRGO
Air + Type A	= LIBRA
Air + Type B	= AQUARIUS
Air + Type C	= GEMINI
Water + Type A	= CANCER
Water + Type B	= SCORPIO
Water + Type C	= PISCES

Congratulations, you have
now determined your dog's Sun Sign!

18

Chapter Three: Bach Flower Remedies For Your Dog

What are Bach Flower Remedies?

Dr. Edward Bach was a homeopathic doctor who recognized the unique power flowers could have over the human psyche and psychical body. During his years of practice in England in the late 1800s, he developed thirty-eight flower-based remedies to treat emotions, moods and mental tendencies.

It was his belief that illnesses were always preceded by mood changes, and if a doctor was able to recognize these changes, he could then begin treatment of the disease before the actual onset occurred, thus lessening or halting the effect of the disease. Dr. Bach developed thirty-eight flower-based remedies to aid in the treatment of his patients. Animal lovers have used the doctor's remedies on their animals with often remarkable results. Taken orally, they can significantly improve the emotional state of your dog.

20

Why Should I Use Bach Flower Remedies on My Dog?

Dogs are products of their environment. Canines are often faced with life-challenges that require an extra boost from nature to help them cope. For example, if a dog has grown emotionally attached to a person and then suddenly that person disappears, the dog has no explanation for why his loved one has gone. He may search for her, stop eating and mourn her loss for months or years. Isn't it comforting to know that there are remedies that may help him deal with this pain? While flower remedies are not miracle concoctions and cannot cure all that ails your pup, they can surely help.

21

What is the Connection Between Bach Flower Remedies and the Zodiac?

Dogs, like people, are affected by the world around them. Determining the Sun Sign your dog was born under can give you important insight into how specific signs will handle different circumstances. However, even those members of the Zodiac who characteristically deal with sudden changes in their lives better than others do not have the tools to deal with every life circumstance perfectly. All members of the Zodiac can benefit from Bach Flower remedies. Considering that each dog is an individual, and she/he possesses unique strengths and weaknesses, I have provided the remedy that I feel will help the emotional needs of each member of the Zodiac canine family based on their Sun Sign.

22

How to Prepare and Administer Bach Flower Remedies:

Your first concern should always be targeting the emotional trauma the dog is encountering and administering the appropriate remedy—please feel free to thumb through other Sun Sign remedies to pick and choose. Once you have chosen the appropriate remedy, place two drops of the remedy into a one-ounce dropper bottle. Fill the bottle to three-quarters full with spring water and shake vigorously 108 times. You may give this to your dog by inserting the dropper into the side of your dog's mouth or by putting the remedy right into your dog's water bowl. You may store this for fourteen days in your refrigerator.

Aries

21 March—19 April
THE RAM

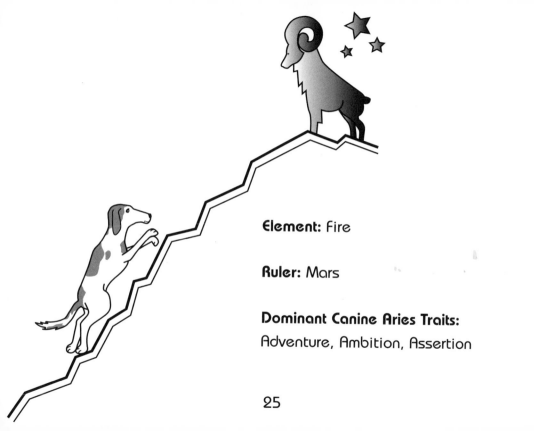

Element: Fire

Ruler: Mars

Dominant Canine Aries Traits:
Adventure, Ambition, Assertion

25

Profile of an Aries Dog:

The Aries dog would make a good
Energizer bunny—he keeps going and going
and going... He will chase his tail until he makes
both himself and you dizzy and delights in any
kind of play. She is a serial face-licker, so keep a box
of tissues handy when you are around her. At

parties, don't be surprised if your pup
manages to get a lampshade stuck on
his head. (And you thought only we nutty
humans did such things!) She is very social and
will greet strangers by nuzzling her nose into their
faces. Her heart is spun from pure gold.

Tail Wagger:

Action. Any way an Aries pooch can let off steam she will take advantage of. She has a tendency to gather up all her energy into a ball and let it loose all over the place! She will zoom around the house in a frenzy—so put away your breakables, step aside and watch her go! If you feel like indulging the kid in yourself and want to join in on the fun, all the better.

Growl:

Leashes. It will take awhile for your Aries dog to get used to being walked on a lead. He will resent being told where to go and when to stop. Never use choke or prong collars on this puppy—he sees them as torture devices. Instead, purchase a nylon harness that fits securely around his torso. This kind of collar will make him feel less like a prisoner and more independent. Treat him as your equal and you will both get along famously.

Training Tip:

Aries dogs are very independent by nature and may be regarded as more difficult to train than other dogs born under different signs. While it is true that their nature makes them appear to be very self-involved, they actually respond to training in a positive way if allowed to retain their sense of self. What that boils down to is this: never yell at an Aries dog or make her

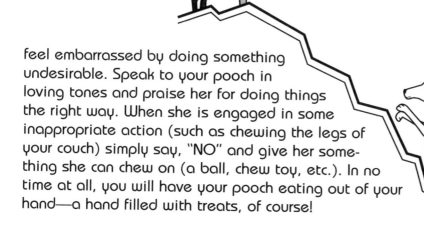

feel embarrassed by doing something undesirable. Speak to your pooch in loving tones and praise her for doing things the right way. When she is engaged in some inappropriate action (such as chewing the legs of your couch) simply say, "NO" and give her something she can chew on (a ball, chew toy, etc.). In no time at all, you will have your pooch eating out of your hand—a hand filled with treats, of course!

Bach Flower Remedy:

Agrimony: For the Aries dog who feels out of sorts when separated from her pack family (you). This remedy will provide her with a sense of security while traveling and is especially useful during trips to the veterinarian.

Boredom Zapper:

A doggie door (into a fenced yard) will not only give your Aries a backyard to play in but will give him the opportunity to relieve himself without waiting for you or the dogwalker to show up.

Favorite Hangout:

In the middle of your living room with all eyes fixed on him.

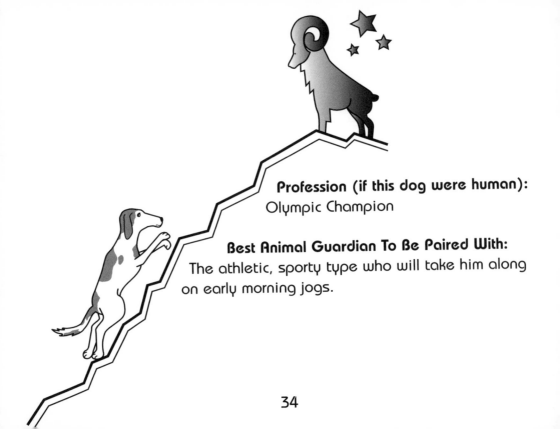

Profession (if this dog were human):
Olympic Champion

Best Animal Guardian To Be Paired With:
The athletic, sporty type who will take him along on early morning jogs.

34

Favorite Quote

"The great pleasure of a dog is that you may make a fool of yourself with him and not only will he not scold you, but he will make a fool of himself too."

-Samuel Butler

Taurus

20 April—20 May
THE BULL

Element: Earth

Ruler: Venus

Dominant Canine Taurus Traits:
Stubbornness, Intelligence, Reliability

Profile of a Taurus Dog:

Dogs born under the Taurus Sun Sign tend to be level-headed and even-keeled. Their behavior does not often go to extremes, and they possess a comforting aura of calm. It takes a lot to get a rise out of them and they tend to act as a neutralizing

presence in times of stress. They are ideal companions for the elderly and physically/mentally challenged.

Tail Wagger:

This sweet-natured pup is his most content snuggling before a warm fire with his family. He enjoys the simple pleasures in life, such as long walks and quiet evenings with his pack family. Offer him tenderness, and he will offer you his heart.

Growl:

Change. Taurus dogs are creatures of habit in the truest sense of the word. Change causes them to feel nervous and unsettled. Family vacations that require her being left behind at a kennel could signal an anxiety attack the size of Texas—best to leave her with a responsible family member she knows or, better yet, just take her along with you!

Training Tip:

Out of all the members of the Zodiac canine family, Taurus dogs are one of the best around children. However, there are always incidents that could occur that you should be aware. For example, children have a habit of pouncing on dogs while they sleep in order to wake them. Such a rude awakening is often greeted with a growl. It is her way of saying, "Stop it, leave me alone."

42

Caution your children to approach a dog quietly and carefully. Allow the dog to sniff their hands and then have the child offer the dog a treat. Very soon, your child will be your dog's best friend. Of course, until you are sure, always have supervised visits between the two for both your child and your dog's safety.

Bach Flower Remedy:

Aspen: Quiets troubling fears that can cause her tail to hang low between her legs. Encourages strength.

Boredom Zapper:

Napping is one way that dogs relieve boredom, so why not make it an enjoyable experience. Go to your local pet supply shop and buy him the softest doggie bed you can find.

Favorite Hangout:

Watching over any person or animal in the house that needs looking after (a newborn, an injured bird, someone in the family who is home sick, etc.). On days when the house is empty, you just may spy your little friend lovingly carrying a stuffed animal in his mouth, tucking it under his favorite pillow.

Profession (if this dog were human):

Nurse

Best Animal Guardian To Be Paired With:

Librarian-types are the perfect match for a Taurus pup because she would enjoy nothing more than being read to in bed. Party animals and swingin' singles would not be her cup of tea—they surround themselves with too much drama for this calm canine.

Favorite Quote:

"Outside of a dog, a book is a man's best friend and inside a dog, it's too dark to read."
　　　-Groucho Marx

47

Gemini

20 May—21 June
THE TWINS

Element: Air

Ruler: Mercury

Dominant Canine Gemini Traits:
Alertness, Intelligence, People-friendly

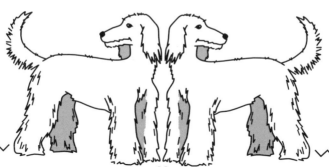

Profile of a Gemini Dog:

Gemini dogs are born hams. Give her an audience
and she will roll over, dance on her hind legs and
howl at the moon just for show. She is a sweet,
kind-hearted pooch who will do just about anything
to see you smile. Whether she is the size of a
Pomeranian or a Great Dane, she always appears

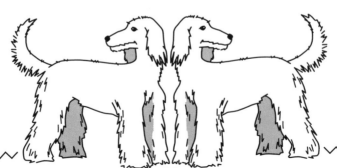

larger than life because her heart extends far enough for everyone to feel its warmth. Her knowing stare will invite you to confess your deepest secrets to her and her mannerisms will assure you that she understands every word.

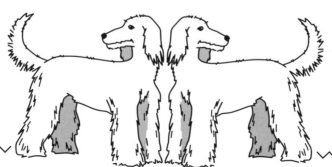

Tail Wagger:

Shadowing. Gemini dogs enjoy following their favorite guardian around the house like a shadow. She will happily prance after you as you answer the door, mow your lawn, vacuum the carpet, etc. Her "hobby" knows no boundaries, so don't be surprised if she follows you right into the shower (especially during scary thunderstorms!)

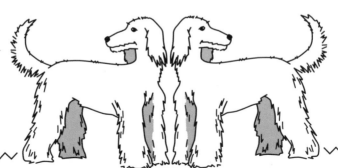

Growl:

Sharing. While Gemini dogs enjoy the company of other dogs, they can be very possessive over their toys. Be sure to have plenty of balls, chew toys, etc.—there must always be enough to go around. If not, you will hear a lot of growling (or worse) coming from your darling Gemini's puppy lips.

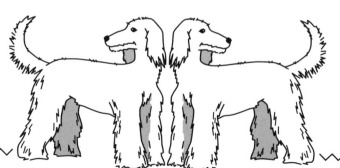

Training Tip:

Gemini dogs are prone to mouthing. Most dogs outgrow mouthing (biting, tugging at people with their mouth) as puppies, but some dogs, such at Gemini, continue this behavior into adulthood. One way to discourage this behavior is to not allow your dog to play Tug-of-War with you. This game confuses your pup into thinking that it is okay to grab hold of

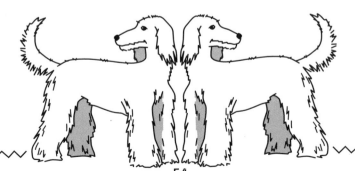

something and not let go. It is difficult for your dog to distinguish between when you are playing the game with him and when he has grabbed hold of something you want to get back from him. When your dog does grab hold of something, firmly tell him, "NO" and replace it with something appropriate for him to chew on.

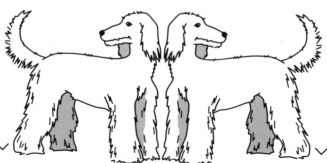

Bach Flower Remedy:

Elm: Encourages the calm after the storm. Sometimes Gemini gets himself all worked up and exhausts himself. This remedy will unfrazzle his nerves.

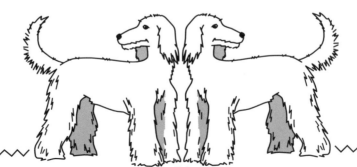

Boredom Zapper:

Tennis balls. Gemini dogs like to pretend that balls are really alive. They will place the balls on the ground, eye it suspiciously and then pounce on it for no apparent reason. A ball can occupy your pooch for hours, so long as it does not roll under the dreaded couch.

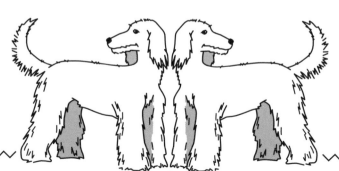

Favorite Hangout:

In the kitchen, scouting for crumbs or other fun things to chew on.

Profession (if this dog were human):

(Soap Opera) Actor

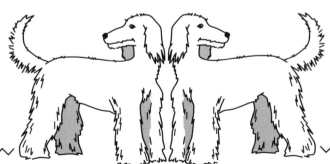

Best animal guardian to be paired with:
Drama Queens come on down and adopt this little
dreamboat! People who surround themselves with
excitement on any level will mesmerize this dog.

Favorite Quote:
"A dog is not "almost human", and I know of no greater
insult to the canine race than to describe it as such."
-John Holmes

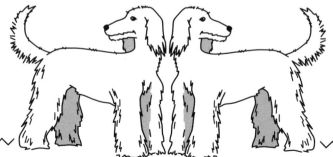

Cancer

22 June—22 July
THE CRAB

Element: Water

Ruler: Moon

Dominant Canine Cancer Traits:
Sensitivity, Moodiness,
Maternal/Paternal Instincts

61

Profile of a Cancer Dog:

Cancer dogs are natural mothers and fathers and are instinctively gentle with children and the elderly. They are chameleons whose mood can be red hot or as cold as ice. One minute he is jumping on you with such affection that he knocks you over, and the next you

62

are begging him to show you some sign of recognition. Their home is their island, and they are very protective of their surroundings.

63

Tail Wagger:

Pampering. Pamper him with love, food, treats and sweet nothings whispered in his ear, and he will devote his life to being your most loyal companion. Indulge him a little by inviting him to act as your pillow as you watch TV—he will proudly carry the weight of your head (so as long as he is bigger than twenty pounds—be careful not to crush him!)

64

Growl:

Being ignored. Cancer is ruled by his emotions, so begging for food and whining when he doesn't get his way shouldn't come as a big surprise. You may find him sulking under the dining room table if he feels he is being ignored or taken for granted. So, as busy as your day may be, always set aside quality time for your special friend.

Training Tip:

Hollering at any dog is not only wrong for the obvious reasons, but it will never bring you the results you want. When dealing with a Cancer dog, it is imperative to remember that all crabs have shells, and the smallest incident can send a Cancer dog retreating back into it. Therefore, you must go extremely slow when trying to train a Cancer. Repetition of the action you want,

66

coupled with a treat, will bring about positive results. Though you may get bored going over the same thing time and time again, you must remember that dogs were not born with a full vocabulary at their disposal. You try picking up Japanese in one afternoon and see how quickly you understand when to sit, stay and come!

67

Bach Flower Remedy:

Red Chestnut: When dogs are frightened by something, the hair on their back stands straight up. This remedy will help the hairs on his back lay flat. When he is spooked by things he does not understand (such as flags blowing in the wind, reflections in windows, people wearing funny hats, etc.), this will help settle his nerves.

68

Boredom Zapper:
Be sure to have a window perch set up for your Cancer dog to look through. He will gladly sit on it all day, barking at any dog who dares to walk down his street.

Favorite Hangout:
On the most comfortable chair in the house. (Think Archie Bunker.)

69

Profession (if this dog were human):
Stay at Home Mom / Mr. Mom

Best Animal Guardian To Be Paired With:

Nannies. Where there are nannies, there are bound to be children, and a Cancer dog delights in playing with little people—so long as they don't try to ride him like a horse.

Favorite Quote:

"No man can be condemned for owning a dog. As long as he has a dog, he has a friend; and the poorer he gets, the better friend he has."

      -Will Rogers

71

Leo

23 July—22 August
THE LION

Element: Fire

Ruler: Sun

Dominant Canine Leo Traits:
Pride, Confidence, Affection

Profile of a Leo Dog:

Dogs born under the Leo Sun Sign are extremely loyal. In fact, a Leo dog will stay with his favorite guardian through thick and thin...unless of course an exciting dog groomer who happens to have some extra room in their home moves into town.

He has a gleam to his coat and will look at you directly in the eye. His charm captivates all who come in contact with him. She is the "show-off" sign of the Zodiac. She enjoys being the boss and will insist on being the leader of the pack. You may pay the bills, but it is your dog who owns the house.

Tail Wagger:

Calming massage. Yes, dogs enjoy getting a gentle massage as much as you do. Stroking, kneading and gentle manipulation of their muscles after a long day at the park can do wonders for his psyche. Start at the base of your Leo's magnificent tail, avoiding direct contact with his spine, and work your way up his back to his neck, gently kneading in a circular motion. In no time at all, your Leo will be collapsed on his back yawning, stretching and looking like the King he is!

Growl:

Silly haircuts. Some dog fanciers insist on shaving bizarre designs into the coat of their dogs. While a Leo dog will gladly sit quite still for a diamond studded collar fitting and allow you to comb out her luxurious hair while placing ribbons and bows on it, she will draw the line at puffy doggie hair-do's. They yearn to hear words of praise as they strut down the street but will become mortally wounded by snickers or snide remarks.

Training Tips:

When dealing with Leo royalty, you must do your best to position yourself as the leader of the pack. This is the ONLY way you will earn a Leo's respect. For you to be perceived as the leader of his pack, you must never allow him to enter or exit through a doorway ahead of you. Dogs in the wild walk in the order of their pack.

Mealtime is an ideal time to show your dominance. While your Leo is eating, handle his food in such a way as to say, "This may be your food, but I am going to stick my hands in it." This will teach him to not be possessive of his food and will further ingrain in his brain that it is you, and not he, who is the leader of your pack family.

Bach Flower Remedy:

Impatiens: A jealous, overbearing, dramatic Leo dog will benefit greatly from this particular remedy when faced with situations beyond his control. Life challenges that make him feel insecure, such as the arrival of a new baby or a new animal companion coming into his castle, will require a little time, patience and a dose of impatiens to settle his nerves.

Boredom Zapper:
Provide your Leo with a radio to listen to while you are away. She prefers pop stations to classical and will enjoy the "company".

Favorite Hangout:
In front of the largest mirror in your house (gazing longingly into his beautiful dog eyes).

Profession (if this dog were human):
Popstar

Best Animal Guardian To Be Paired With:
Costume designers and other behind-the-scenes theater
people would make an excellent match for
this star dog. Who else would bring home
props, tiaras and glittery fabric swatches
for this dog to adorn himself with?

Favorite Quote:

"Heaven goes by favor. If it were by merit, you would stay out and your dog would go in."
                    -Mark Twain

Virgo

23 August—22 September
THE VIRGIN

Element: Earth

Ruler: Mercury

Dominant Canine Virgo Traits:
Sensuousness, Serenity, Empathy

85

Profile of a Virgo Dog:

Virgo canines can best be described as four legged angels who have donned dog suits and swooped down from heaven to bring joy into the world. They intuitively understand your every mood and often mirror your emotions. A Virgo pup loves order. She will expect to be walked, fed and entertained at very specific times...so don't let your punctual pooch down!

Virgo dogs are born healers who embrace life. His natural ability to adapt to almost any situation makes him one of the sweetest dogs of the Zodiac with which to share your life.

Tail Wagger:

Watching television. Don't be surprised to see your little Virgo sitting attentively in front of the television intently watching a nature show or sports program. He enjoys watching images, such as footballs, being tossed across the screen. It may be hard to hold back a chuckle when a tennis match is on—his cute, furry head darting back and forth is quite a sight to see!

Growl:

Visits to the Vet. Since Virgos are hyper-sensitive to their environment, they can empathize with any pain and suffering they experience. Try to make vet visits more casual by arranging for the receptionists and vet assistants to give your dog a treat on days when he does not have an appointment. He will soon learn that while the vet can be an uncomfortable place to be, it can also have benefits such as treats and kind greetings associated with it.

Training Tip:

Virgo dogs know how to forgive, but they seldom forget. Therefore, one mistake in your approach could have disastrous after-affects. When training your Virgo, always begin each session with the basics (sit, stay, come, etc.). This will help ease him into learning new "commands".

Beginning each session with the easiest commands he knows and rewarding him for them will start things off on a positive note (giving him the self-confidence he needs to learn even more).

Bach Flower Remedy:

Centaury: This is an ideal remedy for dogs who put their human's needs before their own. It will give your Virgo canine the extra boost of strength he needs to consider his own well-being as well as his human family. It will benefit him in that it will make him more mindful of grooming his coat, finishing all his food and taking time out of his day to relax and breathe easier.

Boredom Zapper:

Perhaps there is a retired person in your neighborhood whom you trust well enough to enter your home when you are out. If so, it would be beneficial to both that person and your lonesome pooch to get in some socializing during their quiet afternoons. I'll bet that every building or neighborhood has people who would gladly visit lonely dogs during the day, not only for the dog's sake, but for their own needs as well.

Favorite Hangout:

Nose pressed against the window quietly watching the sun set.

Profession (if this dog were human):

Analyst

Best Animal Guardian To Be Paired With:

An elderly or physically challenged human would reap the benefits of sharing his home with such a sensitive Virgo soul. This dog would take great pride in being a companion to someone with special needs.

Favorite Quote:

"If a dog will not come to you after having looked you in the face, you should go home and examine your conscience."
-Woodrow Wilson

Libra

23 September—23 October
THE SCALES

Element: Air

Ruler: Venus

Dominant Canine Libra Traits:
Pushiness, Charm, Intelligence

Profile of a Libra Dog:

Libra dogs receive their greatest pleasure from making their people happy. Because he places such high value on his family, he is the sort of dog that will pace and whine at your door while anxiously awaiting your return. (Even if you are just down the street putting a quarter in the meter!) Virgo will be the most joyful member of your family when you finally come home.

98

He is one of the most agreeable signs of the Zodiac. He is the kind of pooch you can bring to your relative's house for get-togethers without worrying about him "marking up" their house with urine or chewing their furniture. She has often been described as the "Lucky Charm of the Zodiac."

Tail Wagger:

Food. Libra dogs love to eat. She likes nothing better than sitting at the dinner table with you as you throw pieces of bread and pasta into her open mouth. However, you must give her human food treats in moderation as she is prone to obesity.

Growl:

Loneliness. This poor pooch loathes time spent alone. He will lay his body firmly across the doorway until his guardian is safely back at home. Your abode will be fiercely guarded by your Libra, and anyone unfamiliar will have to get through him first if they plan on entering your home illegally.

Training Tip:

Fortunately for you, Libra dogs are quick studies because they will do just about anything for a morsel of food. Be sure not to hand out treats too generously, or they will lose their meaning. When training, treats must always serve as a reward—make him work for it a little.

Always keep the treat in your pup's line of vision by placing it between your pointer and index finger while leading her to do the action you are trying to convey (such as sit and lay down). She is a very intelligent dog, so keep those treats a-comin'!

Bach Flower Remedy:

Rescue Remedy: By far the most popular remedy used by animal lovers. This special combination of Rock Rose, Cherry Plum, Clematis, Impatiens and Star of Bethlehem can aid all members of the Zodiac canine family at one time or another. It is especially useful for high-stress, emergency situations such as moving or a death in the family.

Boredom Zapper:

Why not turn on the television for your pup when the house is empty? Some animal supply stores even carry videos made just for dogs. Television can never replace human contact, but it can be a good distraction for him until you come home.

Favorite Hangout:

In the kitchen, seated lovingly next to his most beloved doggie bowl.

Profession (if this dog were human):

Food Critic

Best Animal Guardian To Be Paired With:

Someone who specializes in home-made doggie treats would be the ideal companion for this Libra, but he really isn't picky. Basically, any dog person who enjoys life to fullest would make this pooch very happy.

106

Favorite Quote:

"Old age means realizing you will never own all the dogs you wanted to."

-Joe Gomes

107

Scorpio

24 October—21 November
THE SCORPION

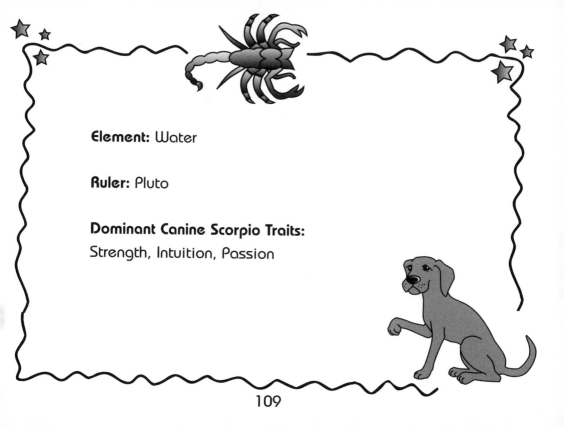

Element: Water

Ruler: Pluto

Dominant Canine Scorpio Traits:
Strength, Intuition, Passion

Profile of a Scorpio Dog:

The Scorpio canine is ruled by her emotions but does not feel very comfortable showing how she feels. She is a complicated enigma. Legend goes, "Look into a Scorpio dog's eyes, and see your soul revealed."

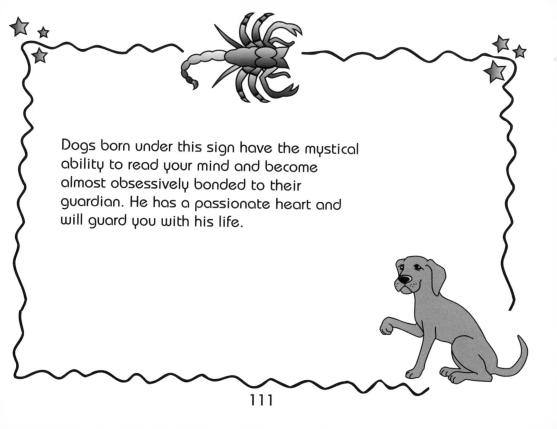

Dogs born under this sign have the mystical ability to read your mind and become almost obsessively bonded to their guardian. He has a passionate heart and will guard you with his life.

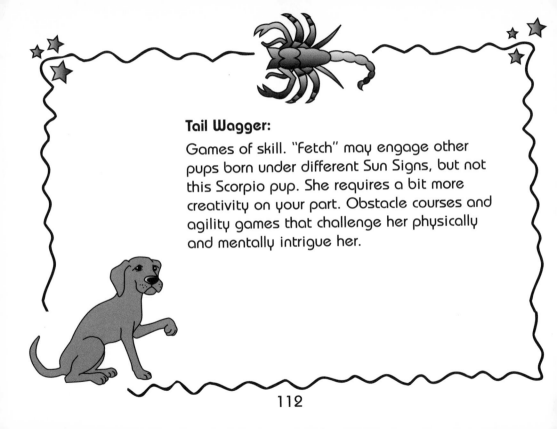

Tail Wagger:

Games of skill. "fetch" may engage other pups born under different Sun Signs, but not this Scorpio pup. She requires a bit more creativity on your part. Obstacle courses and agility games that challenge her physically and mentally intrigue her.

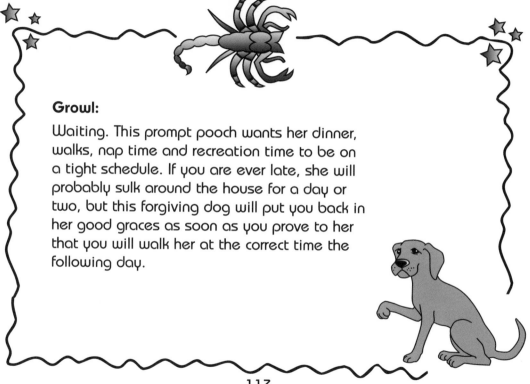

Growl:

Waiting. This prompt pooch wants her dinner, walks, nap time and recreation time to be on a tight schedule. If you are ever late, she will probably sulk around the house for a day or two, but this forgiving dog will put you back in her good graces as soon as you prove to her that you will walk her at the correct time the following day.

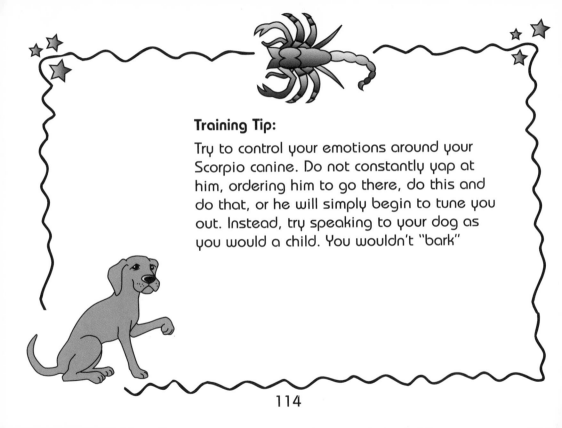

Training Tip:

Try to control your emotions around your Scorpio canine. Do not constantly yap at him, ordering him to go there, do this and do that, or he will simply begin to tune you out. Instead, try speaking to your dog as you would a child. You wouldn't "bark" orders at a youngster, so please monitor your behavior around your dog. Keep in mind, it is usually the human who needs to work on his communication skills, not the other way around.

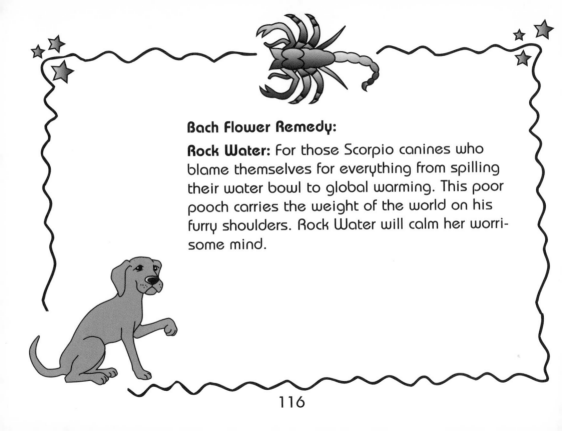

Bach Flower Remedy:

Rock Water: For those Scorpio canines who blame themselves for everything from spilling their water bowl to global warming. This poor pooch carries the weight of the world on his furry shoulders. Rock Water will calm her worrisome mind.

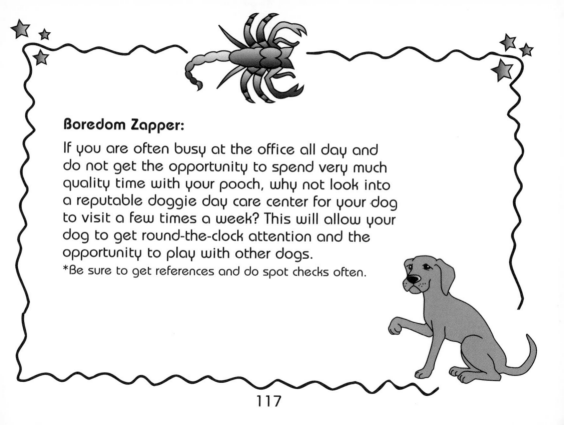

Boredom Zapper:

If you are often busy at the office all day and do not get the opportunity to spend very much quality time with your pooch, why not look into a reputable doggie day care center for your dog to visit a few times a week? This will allow your dog to get round-the-clock attention and the opportunity to play with other dogs.

*Be sure to get references and do spot checks often.

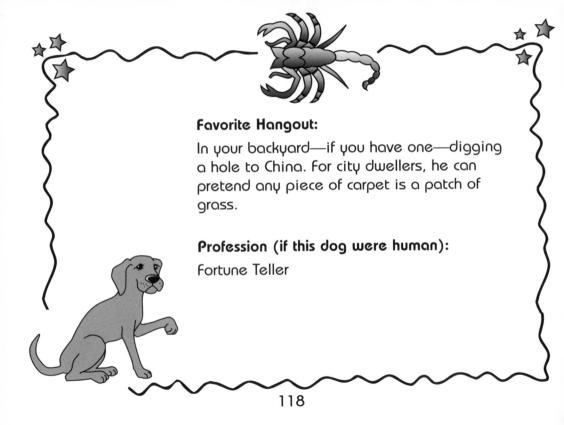

Favorite Hangout:

In your backyard—if you have one—digging a hole to China. For city dwellers, he can pretend any piece of carpet is a patch of grass.

Profession (if this dog were human):

Fortune Teller

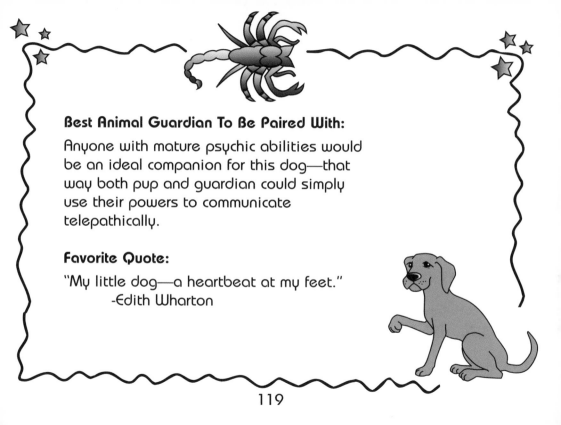

Best Animal Guardian To Be Paired With:

Anyone with mature psychic abilities would be an ideal companion for this dog—that way both pup and guardian could simply use their powers to communicate telepathically.

Favorite Quote:

"My little dog—a heartbeat at my feet."
-Edith Wharton

Sagittarius

22 November—21 December
THE ARCHER

Element: Fire

Ruler: Jupiter

Dominant Canine Sagittarius Traits:
Cheerfulness, Playfulness, Adventure

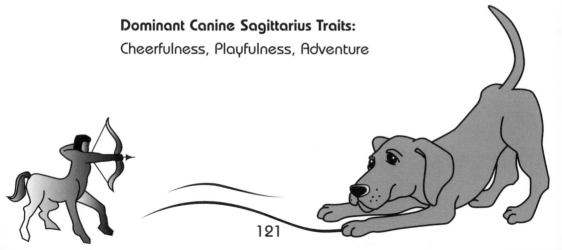

121

Profile of a Sagittarius Dog:

Sagittarius dogs adore the great outdoors and befriend every creature (human or otherwise) who crosses their path. She is so full of energy that spending hours licking your face will not only become her most treasured hobby but will be her honor and privilege.

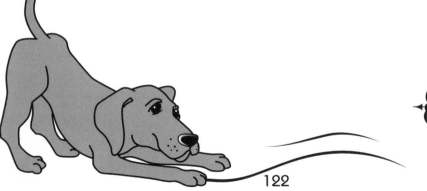

His ability to occupy himself by chasing flies, jumping at shadows cast by the sun and marveling at airplanes is a mesmerizing sight to see.

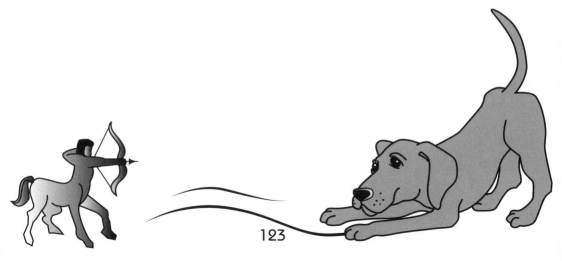

Tail Wagger:

Oral gratification. Chewing, biting
(objects, not people) and licking rank high on
Sagittarius dog's list of favorite pastimes. Give him
one of those doggie cookie jars that allows him to
pull the lever himself whenever he wants a treat,
and he will be your friend forever.

Growl:

Ornaments. While Leo dogs adore being dressed up in elaborate costumes on special occasions such as Halloween, this Sagittarius feels restricted by dog clothing and, quite frankly, a bit goofy. Doggie sweaters, rain slickers, hats, coats and doggie T-shirts make jumping and running a bit uncomfortable for this high-energy pup. Only if the weather drops below freezing will you be able to convince your pooch to wear his coat.

Training Tip:

While you will have to be mindful that she does not chew on dangerous household items such as electrical wires, her chewing will not become a problem so long as you have lots of chew toys available for her to chomp on.

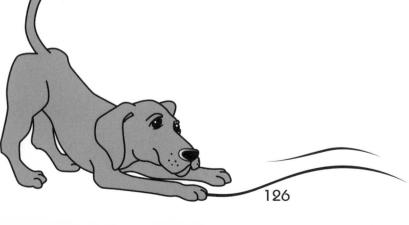

FYI: If your pup does become interested in chewing on live wires, try this simple trick. Go to your local pet supplier and purchase a solution of "Bitter Apple"—a nasty tasting spray that you can apply on potentially fatal chewables. One lick of Bitter Apple will send your dog running. This drastic training trick should only be used in life or death situations.

Bach Flower Remedy:

Wild Oat: For restless Sagittarius souls. Her overactive drive can cause frustrating feelings of boredom and self-pity. This remedy will calm her frantically beating heart and soothe her nerves.

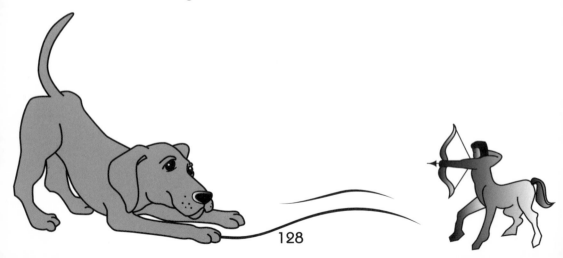

Boredom Zapper:

Dog suppliers produce nylon bones that take a long time for dogs to make a dent in. Sagittarius dogs may spend hours trying to break this nylon bone down.

Favorite Hangout:

Save your money and don't bother to buy her a doggie bed—she will only be happy tucked away under the covers in bed with you.

Profession (if this dog were human):
Butler/Hostess

Best Animal Guardian To Be Paired With:
An outdoorsy type of guy or gal companion who would take time out of his/her day to invite their favorite Sagittarius pooch to join him/her on early morning hikes, walks and bike trips (dog running along side, not actually on the bike) would make this pup's heart sing.

Favorite Quote:
"To err is human: To forgive, canine"
      -Anonymous

131

Capricorn

22 December—19 January
THE GOAT

Element: Earth

Ruler: Saturn

Dominant Canine Capricorn Traits:
Ambition, Intelligence, Loyalty

133

Profile of an Capricorn Dog:

Capricorn canines are old souls. They are very enlightened beings who understand the law of karma. They understand that every action causes a reaction and are mindful to treat others as they themselves wish to be treated. Even as young puppies, they are often the first to move away from their mother to go off and explore

134

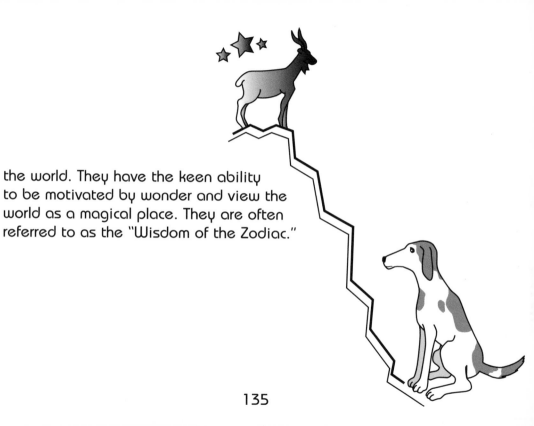

the world. They have the keen ability
to be motivated by wonder and view the
world as a magical place. They are often
referred to as the "Wisdom of the Zodiac."

135

Tail Wagger:

Light dancing. Laser pointers and flash lights pointed on the ground and walls can be a source of great fun for energetic Capricorn dogs. Simply shine the laser on the ground (careful not to aim it at their eyes) and watch your playmate act like a madman as he tries to capture the evasive light. It is one of the only games that will engage him for hours on end.

Growl:

Fourth of July. Why would any dog dislike Independence Day? Are Capricorns anarchists at heart? Unfortunately, fireworks are loud, confusing and frightening things that light up the sky and send your poor pooch running for cover. Closing all your windows, drawing the shades and putting on the air conditioner to shut out the sounds may help calm both of you down.

Training Tip:

It takes a lot of simple, well thought out preparation to condition one of the most intelligent signs of the Zodiac. However, you can train Capricorn effectively if you use your noodle correctly. For example, if your smart Capricorn likes to raid the house for things to destroy, you will have to outsmart him.

Here is a handy pointer that you can try: if she enjoys jumping up on your kitchen counter, try rigging it! Fill some Styrofoam cups filled with pennies and place them just off the side of the counter. Your mischievous Capricorn will eventually knock over the cup, causing it to make a big sound and a small mess. This will instill in her mind that counters tops should be left alone.

Bach Flower Remedy:

Mimulus: Easily unnerved, this Capricorn dog can give himself an ulcer worrying about his family, his home and where his next meal is coming from. When his family quarrels or shows signs of depression, you can usually find your Capricorn camped out under a rug with his paws covering his eyes. This remedy helps to give him the strength he needs to remain calm in a crazy world.

Boredom Zapper:

Why not go down to the local shelter and adopt a playmate for your pooch? Not only will you be saving a life, but your dog (who IS a pack animal) would be so much happier with someone to play with all day.

141

Favorite Hangout:

Sitting on the couch next to you as you speak on the phone. Have you ever noticed that your dog acts animated and excited when you are on the phone? Did you ever wonder why just when you settle in for a heart-to-heart with a friend, your pup suddenly starts to bark and cause a commotion? Well, Silly, that's because he thinks you are speaking to him, and he is just trying to keep up his side of the conversation!

Profession (if this dog were human):
Buddhist Scholar

Best Animal Guardian To Be Paired With:
A child. This very gentle dog will make the perfect companion for your offspring.

Favorite Quote:
"The more one gets to know men, the more one values dogs."
   -Toussenel

143

Aquarius

20 January—18 February
THE WATER BEARER

Element: Air

Ruler: Uranus

Dominant Canine Aquarius Traits:
Aloofness, Adaptability, Curiosity

Profile of an Aquarius Dog:

Your most treasured Aquarius is a rough'n'tumble kind of pup. He loves to get all muddy playing in the yard during hot summer days, and in the winter you can find her trying to build an igloo in the snow with her nose. She is not a complainer and seldom shines or yelps without cause.

He intuitively knows when you have had a lousy day at the office and can turn your frown upside down with a wag of his tail.

Tail Wagger:

Exploring nature. Aquarius dogs are excellent hiking and camping partners. Though his curiosity can get him into trouble at times—(think Winnie the Pooh with his nose stuck in a bee hive)—he will be ecstatic to hike up a mountain and slide down a hill with you. You will notice that as the winds change this pup's nose is always straight up in the air catching new scents.

Growl:

Packs. Aquarius dogs are loners at heart. While they can develop great fondness for their canine buddies, they prefer to have a one-on-one relationship with their human guardian. They should be socialized frequently so as not to further isolate them from other dogs and should be encouraged to play with other canines. Dogs born under this Sun Sign need individual attention and should only be walked with two other dogs at most.

Training Tip:

This tomboy canine likes to jump on strangers. For dog lovers who think this is cute and adorable, no problem. However, our world is also filled with stuffy types who get upset about getting paw prints on their Armani suits—go figure. So, when faced with these uptight humans, it is always better to have a dog who understands, "Off." For stubborn Aquarius dogs, "shake cans" get the point across

in no time. Fill up an old soda can with pennies and hide the can behind your back. When your pup jumps on you, shake the soda can once and say, "Off." When he jumps off you, give him a kiss and a treat. He would much prefer to get this kind of praise than hear that annoying penny-in-the-can noise anyway.

Bach Flower Remedy:

Crab Apple: Domesticated dogs are often forced to surpress their primal urges. This can break a dog's spirit and an Aquarius pup's heart. Crab apple will give her the incentive to reconnect with her organic aura and embrace her wild side. Don't worry, she won't suddenly become an unmanageable wolf—just don't be alarmed if you see her worshipping, howling and baying at the alter of the moon.

Boredom Zapper:

Kiddie swimming pools are not just for children. Your Aquarius dog would enjoy her summer days so much more if she had a little pool to jump around in.

153

Favorite Hangout:

Standing in your kitchen with her head buried deep in the garbage can. You know what they say, "One man's garbage is another dog's snack!"

Profession (if this dog were human):
World Traveler

Best Animal Guardian To Be Paired With:

Anyone who enjoys boating would be a match made in heaven for this Aquarius water-bearing dog, but all this dog truly requires is someone who is in touch with their spiritual side. They bond closely with those who have retained their child-like sense of wonder about the planet they live on.

Favorite Quote:

"When it comes to suffering, a pig is a rat is a dog is a boy."
                    -Ingrid Newkirk

Pisces

19 February—20 March
THE FISH

Element: Water

Ruler: Neptune

Dominant Canine Pisces Traits:
Compassion, Psychic Ability, Creativity

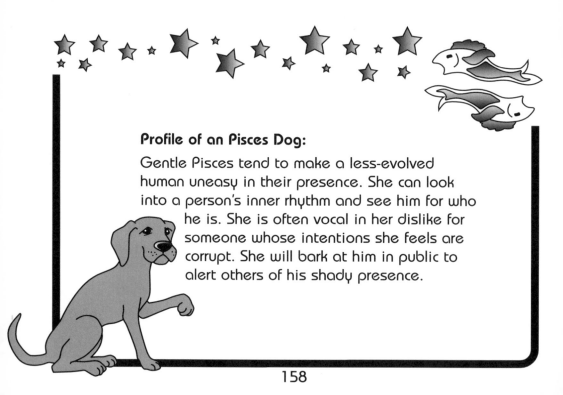

Profile of an Pisces Dog:

Gentle Pisces tend to make a less-evolved human uneasy in their presence. She can look into a person's inner rhythm and see him for who he is. She is often vocal in her dislike for someone whose intentions she feels are corrupt. She will bark at him in public to alert others of his shady presence.

Pisces speak the universal language understood by all—the language of love. She will lean on you and place her head on your knee when you need a little bit of encouragement to get on with your day. They have incredibly soulful eyes and if you gaze at them for too long, you may lose your heart forever.

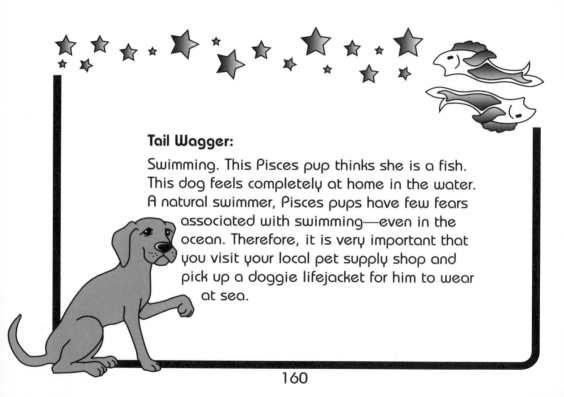

Tail Wagger:

Swimming. This Pisces pup thinks she is a fish. This dog feels completely at home in the water. A natural swimmer, Pisces pups have few fears associated with swimming—even in the ocean. Therefore, it is very important that you visit your local pet supply shop and pick up a doggie lifejacket for him to wear at sea.

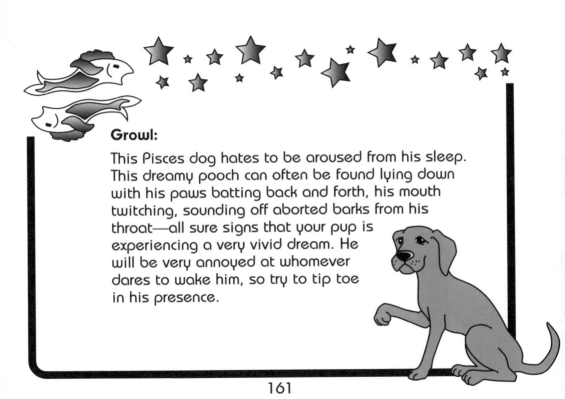

Growl:

This Pisces dog hates to be aroused from his sleep.
This dreamy pooch can often be found lying down
with his paws batting back and forth, his mouth
twitching, sounding off aborted barks from his
throat—all sure signs that your pup is
experiencing a very vivid dream. He
will be very annoyed at whomever
dares to wake him, so try to tip toe
in his presence.

161

Training Tip:

If your Pisces dog becomes so enthralled by the world around him that he forgets to pay attention to you, walking him on a leash can become an issue. They have a tendency to forge ahead on the leash, pulling their human companion behind them. In order to change this behavior it is important to get her to focus on you.

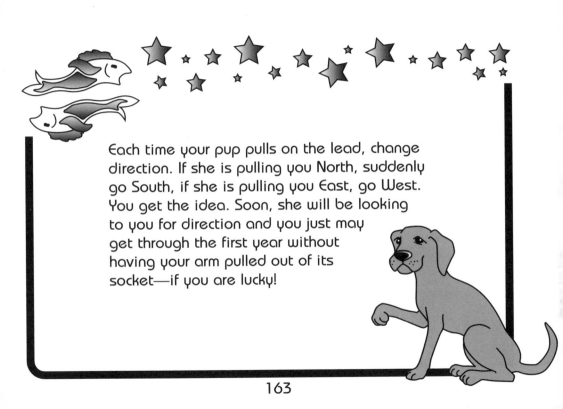

Each time your pup pulls on the lead, change direction. If she is pulling you North, suddenly go South, if she is pulling you East, go West. You get the idea. Soon, she will be looking to you for direction and you just may get through the first year without having your arm pulled out of its socket—if you are lucky!

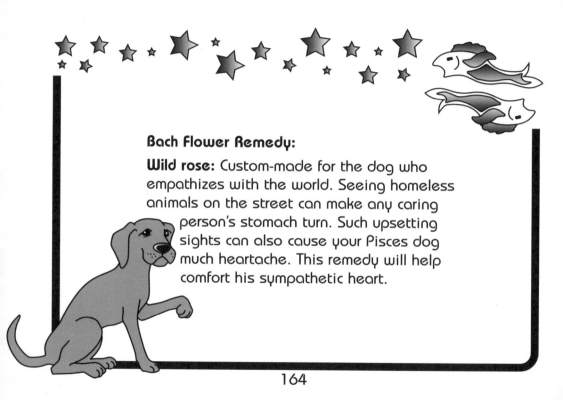

Bach Flower Remedy:

Wild rose: Custom-made for the dog who empathizes with the world. Seeing homeless animals on the street can make any caring person's stomach turn. Such upsetting sights can also cause your Pisces dog much heartache. This remedy will help comfort his sympathetic heart.

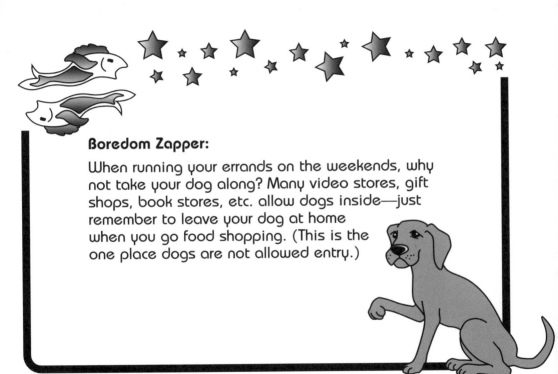

Boredom Zapper:

When running your errands on the weekends, why not take your dog along? Many video stores, gift shops, book stores, etc. allow dogs inside—just remember to leave your dog at home when you go food shopping. (This is the one place dogs are not allowed entry.)

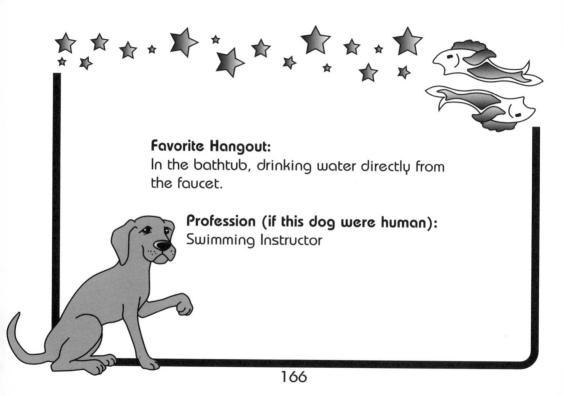

Favorite Hangout:
In the bathtub, drinking water directly from the faucet.

Profession (if this dog were human):
Swimming Instructor

Best Animal Guardian To Be Paired With:
Artistic types. Dogs born under this Sun Sign appreciate wild spirits who will take off the afternoon at the drop of a hat to head to the beach. (With their favorite dog, of course!)

Favorite Quote:
"Dogs love their friends and bite their enemies, quite unlike people who are incapable of pure love and always have to mix love and hate."
                    -Sigmund Freud

Other Titles by Great Quotations

The ABC's of Parenting
African-American Wisdom
As A Cat Thinketh
Astrology for Cats
Astrology for Dogs
The Be-Attitudes
The Best of Friends
The Birthday Astrologer
Can We Talk
Celebrating Women
Chicken Soup
Chocoholic Reasonettes
The Cornerstones of Success
Daddy & Me
Erasing My Sanity
Fantastic Father, Dependable Dad
Global Wisdom
Golden Years, Golden Words
Graduation Is Just The Beginning
Grandma, I Love You
Growing Up in Toyland
Happiness Is Found Along The Way
High Anxieties

Hollywords
Hooked on Golf
I Didn't Do It
I'm Not Over the Hill
Ignorance is Bliss
Inspirations
Interior Design for Idiots
The Lemonade Handbook
Let's Talk Decorating
Life's Lessons
Life's Simple Pleasures
A Lifetime of Love
A Light Heart Lives Long
Looking for Mr. Right
Midwest Wisdom
Mommy & Me
Mother, I Love You
Motivating Quotes
    for Motivated People
Mrs. Murphy's Laws
Mrs. Webster's Dictionary
My Daughter, My Special Friend
Only a Sister

The Other Species
Parenting 101
Reflections
Romantic Rhapsody
The Rose Mystique
The Secret Language of Men
The Secret Language of Women
The Secrets in Your Face
The Secrets in Your Name
Size Counts!
Social Disgraces
Some Things Never Change
The Sports Page
Sports Widow
Stress or Sanity
A Teacher Is Better Than
    Two Books
TeenAge of Insanity
Thanks from the Heart
Things You'll Learn...
Wedding Wonders
Words From The Coach
Working Woman's World

GREAT QUOTATIONS PUBLISHING COMPANY
Glendale Heights, IL 60139
Phone (630) 582-2800 • Fax (630) 582-2813